The Little
SCA
& Arpeggios
For Guitar

E A D G B E

F B♭ E♭ A♭ C F

Exclusive distributors:
Music Sales Limited 8/9 Frith Street, London W1V 5TZ, England.
Music Sales Pty Limited 120 Rothschild Avenue Rosebery, NSW 2018, Australia.

Order No.AM959464 ISBN 0-7119-7454-3
This book © Copyright 1999 by Wise Publications

Unauthorised reproduction of any part of this publication by any means including photocopying
is an infringement of copyright.

Written by Joe Bennett
Book layout, design and music engraving by Simon Troup

Printed in the United Kingdom by Printwise (Haverhill) Limited, Haverhill, Suffolk.

Your Guarantee of Quality
As publishers, we strive to produce every book to the highest commercial standards.
Particular care has been given to specifying acid-free, neutral-sized paper made from pulps which have not been
elemental chlorine bleached. This pulp is from farmed sustainable forests and was produced with special regard
for the environment. Throughout, the printing and binding have been planned to ensure a sturdy, attractive
publication which should give years of enjoyment. If your copy fails to meet our high standards, please inform us
and we will gladly replace it.

Music Sales' complete catalogue describes thousands of titles and is available in full colour sections by subject,
direct from Music Sales Limited. Please state your areas of interest and send a cheque/postal order for £1.50 for
postage to: Music Sales Limited, Newmarket Road, Bury St. Edmunds, Suffolk IP33 3YB.

www.musicsales.com

Wise Publications
London/New York/Sydney/Paris/Copenhagen/Madrid/Tokyo

CONTENTS

Scales - why bother?

None of us picked up the guitar because we liked scales. Learning scales is the musical equivalent of maths homework – you know you have to do it, but that doesn't mean you have to enjoy it, right? But we want to express ourselves through the language of music, and as with any language, to express yourself you need a vocabulary.

When you look at it in this way, scales start to become more of a time-saver than a chore. If you're using the 'right' scale to improvise a solo or play a melody, you're taking all of that random guesswork out of your playing, saving time for the creative stuff.

In this book you'll find all of the most used and useful scales, plus over 40 shapes for arpeggios. When you're playing a solo, you rarely think in terms of scale tones alone – the underlying chord should always be on your mind. So arpeggio shapes, again, are a handy shortcut to the sounds you want to make.

About this book

This pocket guide gives you all the information you need to play over 300 scales. However, we didn't want your guitar case to be weighted down with 150 pages of diagrams, so all the scales are shown in the key of A. Use the fingerboard diagram opposite to figure out the scales in all 12 keys, moving each shape to the relevant fret to change the key.

The scales are shown in four formats - traditional music notation, guitar tablature, guitar fretbox and scale formula. A scale formula refers to the number of the note within the scale you are playing in relation to the interval sequence of the major scale (e.g: 3 = the third, etc).

All the scales and arpeggios are shown in their ascending form only to save space. Each should be played ascending and descending, without repeating the top note.

On page 57, you'll also find some exercises to get you started using scales for soloing. You should be able to play any new scale using these exercises – that's the only way you'll achieve enough fluency to use it meaningfully in a guitar solo.

Fretboard Diagram

Any scale can be played in any of the 12 musical keys - it's simply a question of moving your hand to the right fret position, and finding the scale's root note on one of the diagrams below. Root notes (shown in black circles on the fretboards) give a scale its letter name. So, once you can play a new shape, you've in fact learned 12 scales!

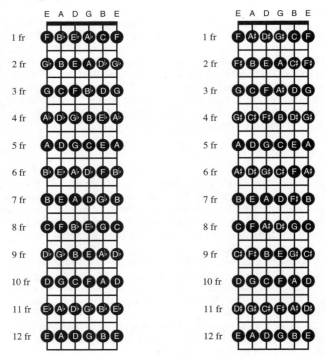

This diagram shows how to find any scale's root note, and will help you if the scale you want has a flat (♭) in its name.

This diagram shows the same information, but using alternate names for the notes. It will help you if the scale you want has a sharp (♯) in its name.

Chord Diagrams Explained

Fretboxes show the guitar on it side, with the headstock, nut and tuning pegs at the left of the picture - six horizontal lines represent the strings.

The 'O' symbol means play the string 'open' without fretting a note.

Vertical lines represent the frets, horizontal lines the strings.

The thick black line represents the nut of the guitar.

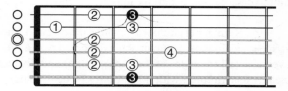

Numbers in a circle show which finger you should use to fret the note.

Numbers shown in black are the 'root' of the chord – *i.e.* its letter name.

Notation and Tablature

'Tab' is drawn with the guitar on its side, with the thickest string at the bottom – the six horizontal lines represent the strings.

The top stave shows the scale as it would appear in traditional music notation.

On the tablature, the numbers represent the fret positions, while the letters underneath the tab show you the actual note names you're playing. A zero means the string should be played open.

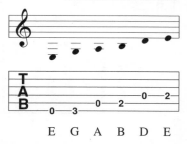

E   G   A   B   D   E

Beginner's scales

For the novice player, this section includes five of the easiest shapes to get you started. All of these are 'open' scales – i.e. they use open strings and fretted notes combined. This gives the advantage that they are easier to play, but unfortunately can only be played in the key shown. Fretted shapes (see page 9 onwards) are more versatile, but generally tougher to play.

Remember, it doesn't matter if you can't play these scales at speed, as long as you can achieve accuracy (i.e. the right notes), evenness (all the notes at the same tempo) and distinctness (i.e. clean, clear fretting, with no fret buzz or bent notes).

Open G major scale
1 2 3 4 5 6 7

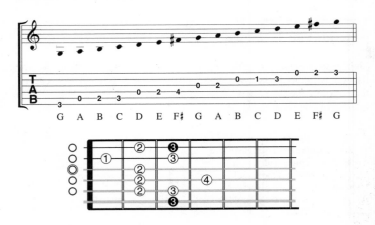

Open C major scale

1 2 3 4 5 6 7

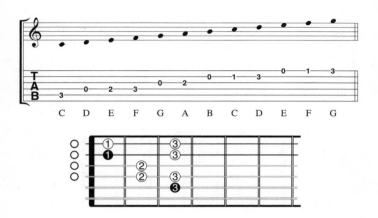

Open E minor pentatonic scale

1 ♭3 4 5 ♭7

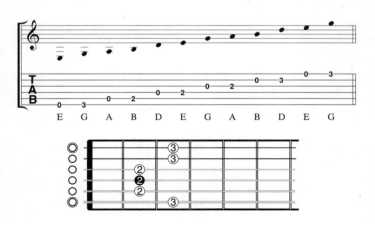

Open E blues scale   1 ♭3 4 ♯4 5 ♭7

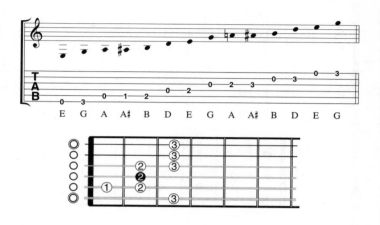

Open G major pentatonic scale   1 2 3 5 6

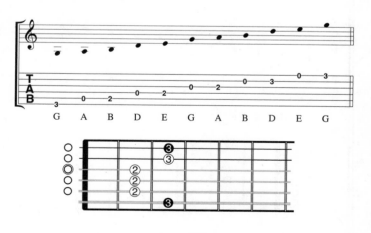

Major scales

The major scale is the most important set of notes in the history of Western music. Almost all of our harmony is based on it, and every one of the 'modes' (including the Natural Minor scale, also known as the Aeolian mode) is derived from its pattern of tones and semitones. In this section the major scale is shown in its easiest fretted position, which can be played using one-finger-per-fret technique, plus the seven positions of three-notes-per-string technique, which is more versatile and gives a broader range of notes.

In the following examples, notes below the root note are greyed out to help you when moving the shape to other keys.

A major scale position 1

1 2 3 4 5 6 7

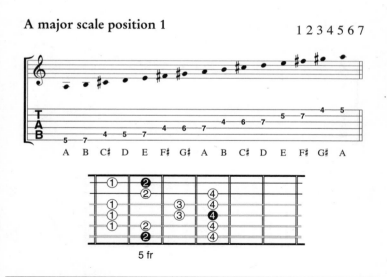

A major scale position 2

1 2 3 4 5 6 7

7 fr

A major scale position 3

1 2 3 4 5 6 7

12 fr

A major scale position 4

1 2 3 4 5 6 7

E F♯ G♯ A B C♯ D E F♯ G♯ A B C♯ D E F♯ G♯

12 fr

A major scale position 5

1 2 3 4 5 6 7

E F♯ G♯ A B C♯ D E F♯ G♯ A B C♯ D E F♯ G♯ A

12 fr

A major scale position 6

1 2 3 4 5 6 7

F♯ G♯ A B C♯ D E F♯ G♯ A B C♯ D E F♯ G♯ A B

17 fr

A major scale position 7

1 2 3 4 5 6 7

G♯ A B C♯ D E F♯ G♯ A B C♯ D E F♯ G♯ A B C♯

17 fr

Minor scales

The Natural Minor scale shown is the one that guitarists use most frequently. It's different from the minor scale you'll find in a grade 1 classical book, which has a sharpened 7th. This 'harmonic minor' can be found on page 27.

All of the minor scales shown below are fretted shapes, so there should be no open strings.

As before, notes below the root note have been greyed out, so to play these in a different key, make sure you use the root note as the starting point, rather than the lowest note.

A minor scale position 1   1 2 ♭3 4 5 ♭6 ♭7

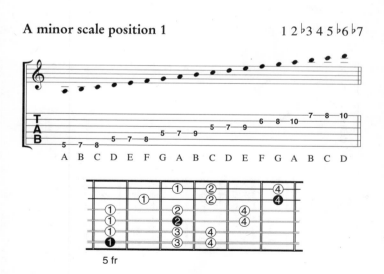

A minor scale position 2

$1\ 2\ \flat3\ 4\ 5\ \flat6\ \flat7$

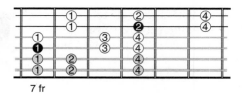

7 fr

A minor scale position 3

$1\ 2\ \flat3\ 4\ 5\ \flat6\ \flat7$

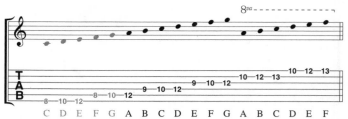

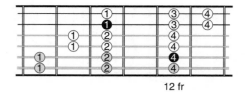

12 fr

A minor scale position 4

1 2 ♭3 4 5 ♭6 ♭7

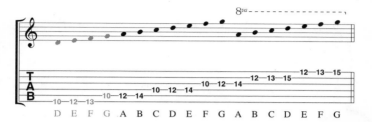

A minor scale position 5

1 2 ♭3 4 5 ♭6 ♭7

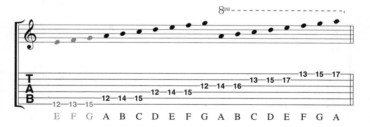

15

A minor scale position 6

1 2 ♭3 4 5 ♭6 ♭7

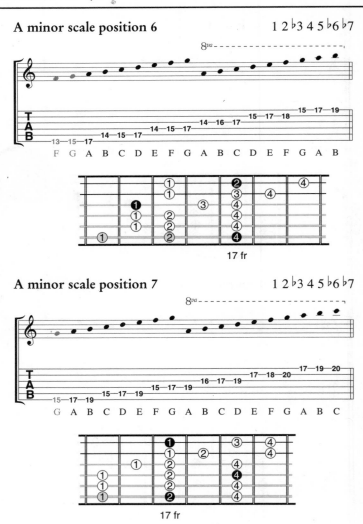

F G A B C D E F G A B C D E F G A B

17 fr

A minor scale position 7

1 2 ♭3 4 5 ♭6 ♭7

G A B C D E F G A B C D E F G A B C

17 fr

Pentatonic scales

Pentatonics are literally '5-note scales', and there are two main types. The Major Pentatonic scale is the major scale with the 4th and 7th missed out. The Minor Pentatonic is the natural minor scale with the 2nd and 6th missed out.

Missing out these notes gives us two advantages. Firstly, pentatonics are usually easier to play. Secondly, because we've missed out the notes which are more likely to clash, any notes we choose to play are more likely to sound 'right' with the backing. In short, if you're in any doubt, use a pentatonic!

A minor pentatonic scale position 1   1 ♭3 4 5 ♭7

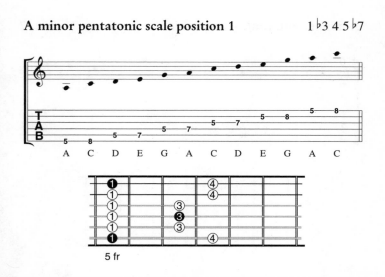

A minor pentatonic scale position 2

1 ♭3 4 5 ♭7

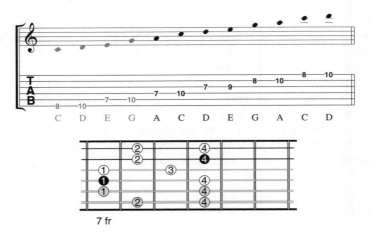

A minor pentatonic scale position 3

1 ♭3 4 5 ♭7

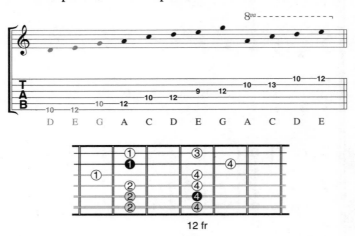

A minor pentatonic scale position 4

1 ♭3 4 5 ♭7

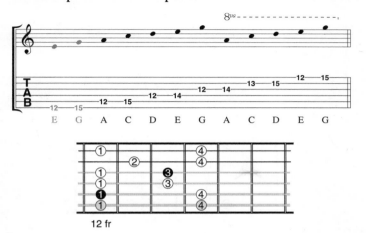

A minor pentatonic scale position 5

1 ♭3 4 5 ♭7

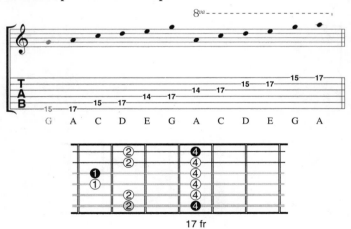

A major pentatonic scale position 1

1 2 3 5 6

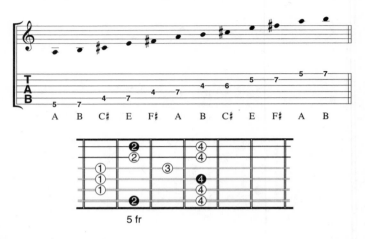

5 fr

A major pentatonic scale position 2

1 2 3 5 6

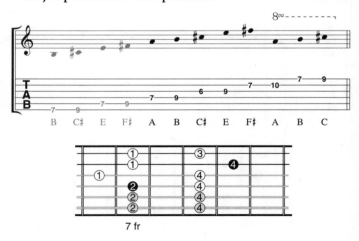

7 fr

A major pentatonic scale position 3

1 2 3 5 6

C♯ E F♯ A B C♯ E F♯ A B C♯ E

12 fr

A major pentatonic scale position 4

1 2 3 5 6

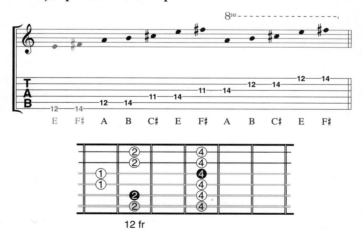

E F♯ A B C♯ E F♯ A B C♯ E F♯

12 fr

A major pentatonic scale position 5

1 2 3 5 6

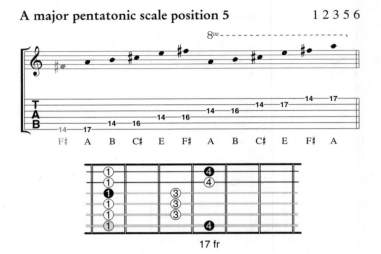

F# A B C# E F# A B C# E F# A

17 fr

Modes and specialist scales

There are seven modes, and they are all based on the intervals of the major scale. In modes, the intervals are played in the same order as in the major scale, but juxtaposed by one note - so for example, if you started playing the notes of A major, but beginning with a B, you would create B Dorian.

For this reason it's easiest to think of each mode as a scale in its own right, and learn separate fingerings and licks accordingly. We've already covered two of the modes – the Ionian (also known as the major scale) and Aeolian (the Natural Minor scale). The remaining five (Dorian, Mixolydian, Phrygian, Lydian and Locrian) are shown in this chapter. Of these, the two most common – Dorian and Mixolydian – are shown in two fingerboard positions.

A dorian mode version 1   1 2 ♭3 4 5 6 ♭7

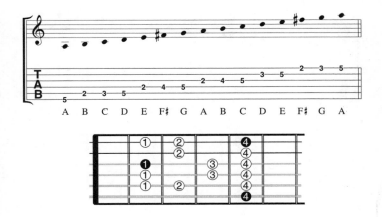

A dorian mode version 2

1 2 ♭3 4 5 6 ♭7

A B C D E F♯ G A B C D E F♯ G A B C D

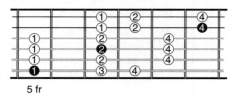

5 fr

A mixolydian mode version 1

1 2 3 4 5 6 ♭7

A B C♯ D E F♯ G A B C♯ D E F♯ G A B

5 fr

A mixolydian mode version 2

1 2 3 4 5 6 ♭7

A B C♯ D E F♯ G A B C♯ D E F♯ G A B C♯ D

5 fr

A phrygian mode

1 ♭2 ♭3 4 5 ♭6 ♭7

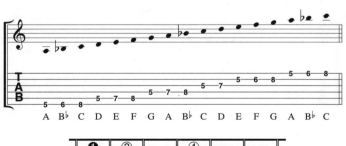

A B♭ C D E F G A B♭ C D E F G A B♭ C

5 fr

A lydian mode

1 2 3 ♯4 5 6 7

A B C♯ D♯ E F♯ G♯ A B C♯ D♯ E F♯ G♯ A B

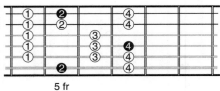

5 fr

A locrian mode

1 ♭2 ♭3 4 ♭5 ♭6 ♭7

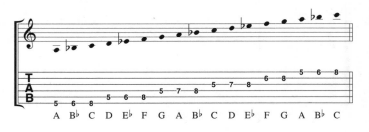

A B♭ C D E♭ F G A B♭ C D E♭ F G A B♭ C

5 fr

A harmonic minor scale

1 2 ♭3 4 5 ♭6 ♯7

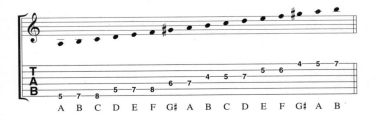

A B C D E F G♯ A B C D E F G♯ A B

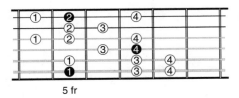

5 fr

A "Jazz" melodic minor

1 2 ♭3 4 5 6 7

A B C D E F♯ G♯ A B C D E F♯ G♯ A B

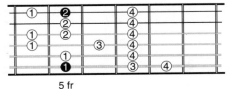

5 fr

A altered scale

$1\ \flat2\ \flat3\ \flat4\ \flat5\ \flat6\ \flat7$

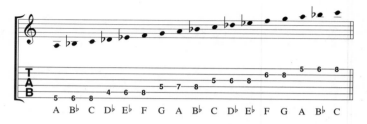

A B♭ C D♭ E♭ F G A B♭ C D♭ E♭ F G A B♭ C

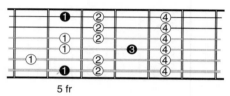

5 fr

A whole tone scale

$1\ 2\ 3\ \sharp4\ \flat6\ \flat7$

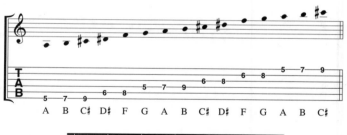

A B C♯ D♯ F G A B C♯ D♯ F G A B C♯

5 fr

A diminished scale

1 2 ♭3 4 ♯4 ♭6 6 7

A B C D D♯ F F♯ G♯ A B C D D♯ F F♯ G♯ A B

5 fr

A lydian ♭7 scale

1 2 3 ♯4 5 6 ♭7

A B C♯ D♯ E F♯ G A B C♯ D♯ E F♯ G A B

5 fr

Arpeggios

What's an arpeggio? When you play all of the notes that occur in a chord separately, one after the other, this is called an arpeggio. Arpeggios are particularly useful for improvising, because if you know the names of the notes in a chord you will always know which notes will 'work' over a given chord backing.

Learning arpeggios is also a great way of getting your playing out of a scalic 'rut' – whoever said that you can't have big leaps in a tune?

In this section, the arpeggios which are less than an octave (majors, minors, 7ths etc) are shown right across the fingerboard – i.e. in several octaves. Those which use extended intervals (9ths, 11ths, 13ths etc) are shown in one position only to avoid confusion. These are just some of the shapes available – there are literally thousands of arpeggios to be found on the guitar fingerboard.

As with the scales, there are open and fretted arpeggios – open ones are easier but less versatile. Each arpeggio is shown ascending only, but should be practised both ascending and descending.

Once again, notes in each shape which occur before the root note are greyed out. When practising, always try to remember where the root note is, as this will make it easier for you to move the shape around the fretboard.

Open C major arpeggio   1 3 5

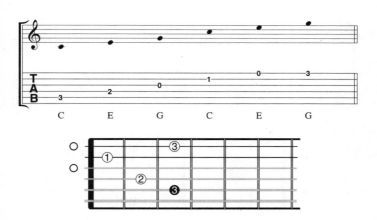

C   E   G   C   E   G

Open A minor arpeggio   1 ♭3 5

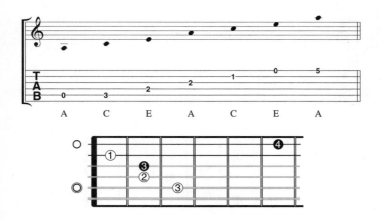

A   C   E   A   C   E   A

A major arpeggio position 1

1 3 5

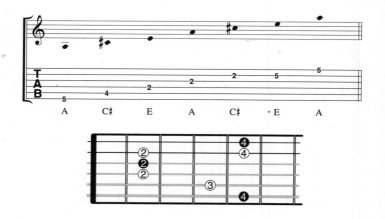

A   C#   E   A   C#   E   A

A major arpeggio position 2

1 3 5

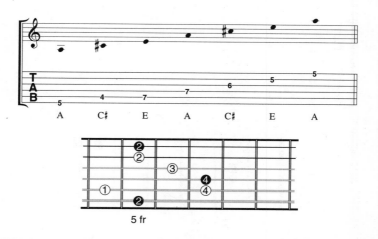

A   C#   E   A   C#   E   A

5 fr

A major arpeggio position 3

1 3 5

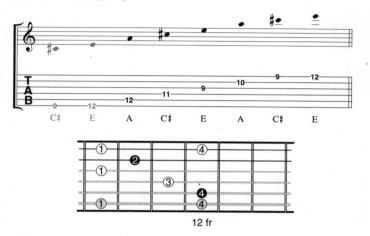

C♯ E A C♯ E A C♯ E

12 fr

A major arpeggio position 4

1 3 5

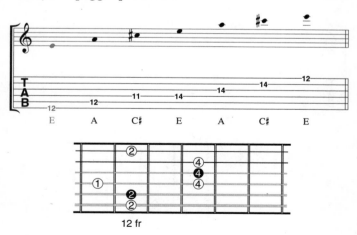

E A C♯ E A C♯ E

12 fr

A minor arpeggio position 1

1 ♭3 5

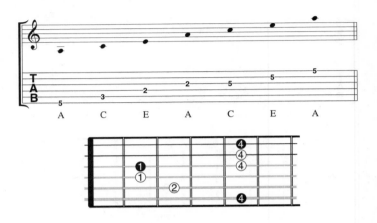

A minor arpeggio position 2

1 ♭3 5

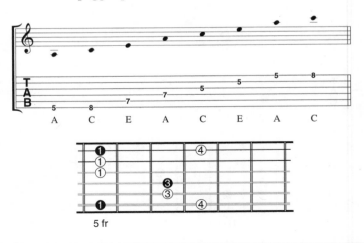

5 fr

A minor arpeggio position 3

1 ♭3 5

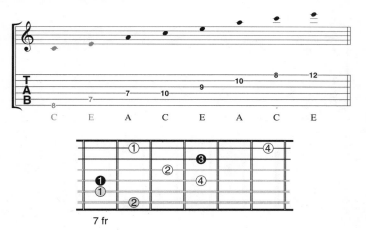

C   E   A   C   E   A   C   E

7 fr

A minor arpeggio position 4

1 ♭3 5

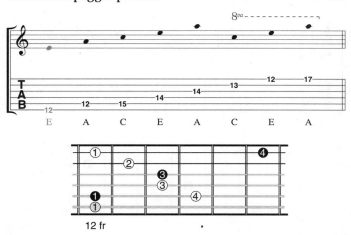

E   A   C   E   A   C   E   A

12 fr

A augmented arpeggio version 1

1 3 #5

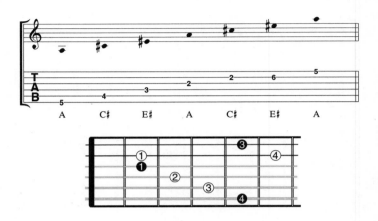

A   C#   E#   A   C#   E#   A

A augmented arpeggio version 2

1 3 #5

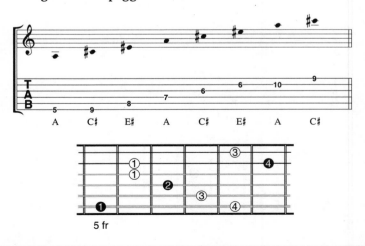

A   C#   E#   A   C#   E#   A   C#

5 fr

A diminished arpeggio version 1

1 ♭3 ♭5 ♭♭7

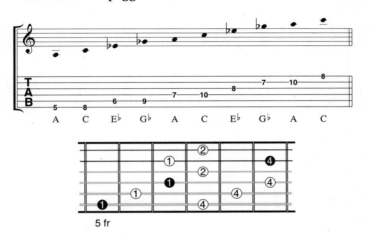

A diminished arpeggio version 2

1 ♭3 ♭5 ♭♭7

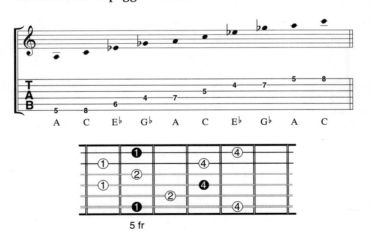

A dominant 7th arpeggio version 1 1 3 5 ♭7

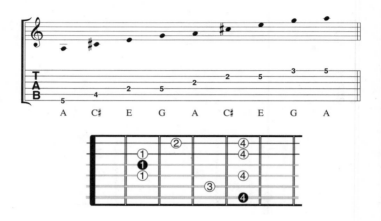

A dominant 7th arpeggio version 2 1 3 5 ♭7

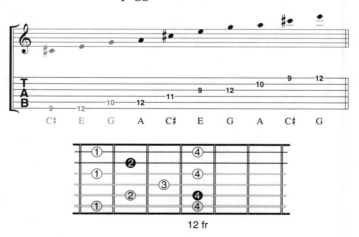

A major 7th arpeggio version 1

1 3 5 7

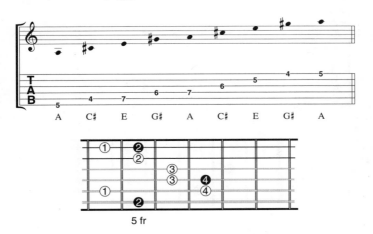

A major 7th arpeggio version 2

1 3 5 7

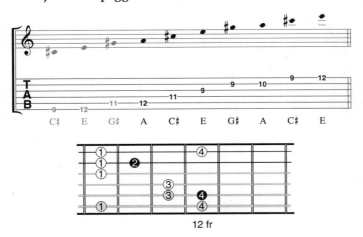

A minor 7th arpeggio version 1

1 ♭3 5 ♭7

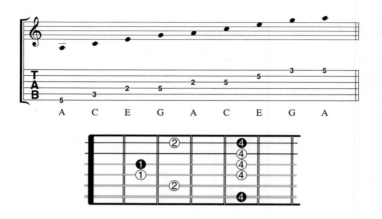

A minor 7th arpeggio version 2

1 ♭3 5 ♭7

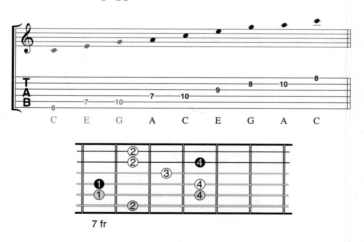

7 fr

A minor (major 7th) arpeggio version 1

1 ♭3 5 7

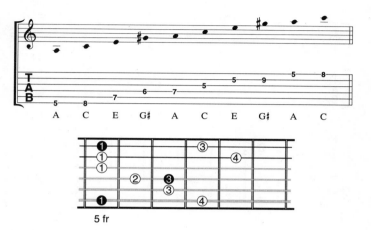

| A | C | E | G♯ | A | C | E | G♯ | A | C |

5 fr

A minor (major 7th) arpeggio version 2

1 ♭3 5 7

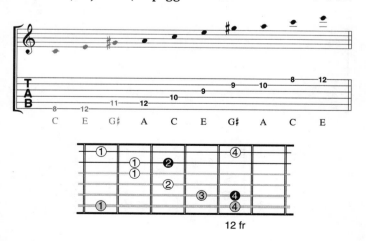

| C | E | G♯ | A | C | E | G♯ | A | C | E |

12 fr

A minor 7th ♭5 arpeggio version 1

1 ♭3 ♭5 ♭7

A   C   E♭   G   A   C   E♭   G   A   C

5 fr

A minor 7th ♭5 arpeggio version 2

1 ♭3 ♭5 ♭7

E♭   G   A   C   E♭   G   A   C   E♭   G

12 fr

42

A major 6th arpeggio version 1   1 3 5 6

A   C♯   E   F♯   A   C♯   E   F♯   A

A major 6th arpeggio version 2   1 3 5 6

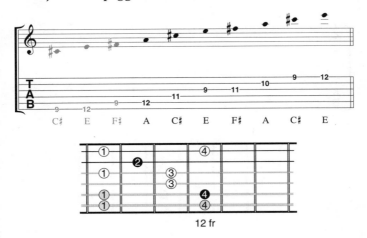

C♯   E   F♯   A   C♯   E   F♯   A   C♯   E

12 fr

A dominant 9th arpeggio version 1   1 3 5 ♭7 9

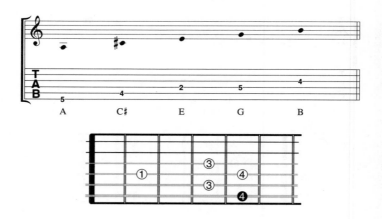

A dominant 9th arpeggio version 2   1 3 5 ♭7 9

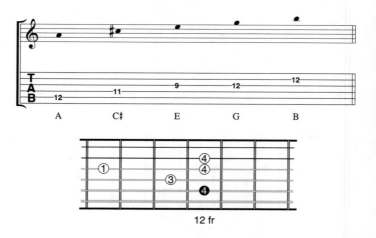

A major 9th arpeggio version 1

1 3 5 7 9

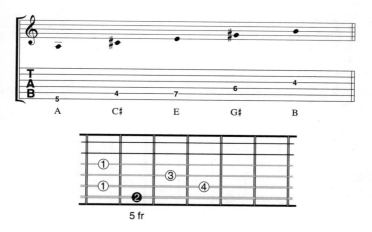

A major 9th arpeggio version 2

1 3 5 7 9

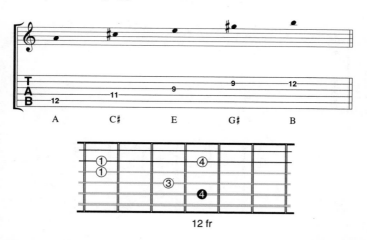

A minor 9th (major 7th) arpeggio version 1   1 ♭3 5 7 9

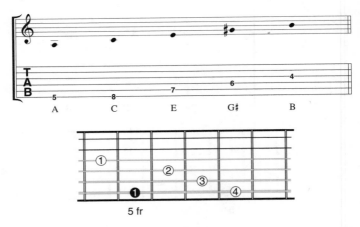

A minor 9th (major 7th) arpeggio version 2   1 ♭3 5 7 9

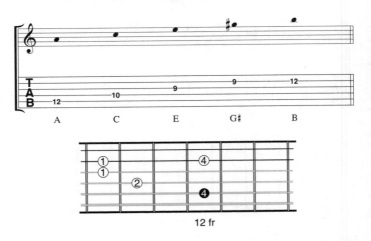

A minor 9th arpeggio version 1

1 ♭3 5 ♭7 9

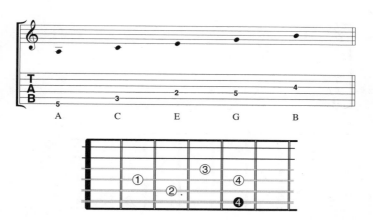

A minor 9th arpeggio version 2

1 ♭3 5 ♭7 9

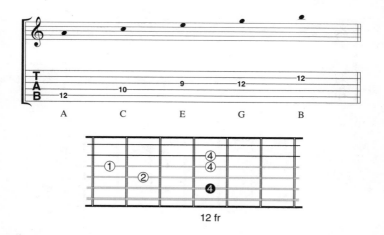

A dominant 11th arpeggio version 1

1 3 5 ♭7 9 11

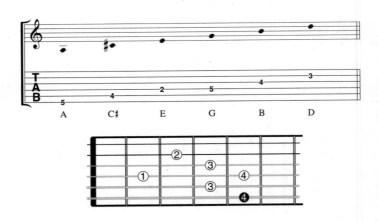

A dominant 11th arpeggio version 2

1 3 5 ♭7 9 11

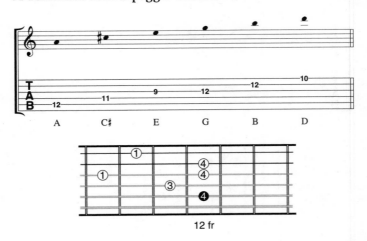

A major 11th arpeggio version 1   1 3 5 7 9 11

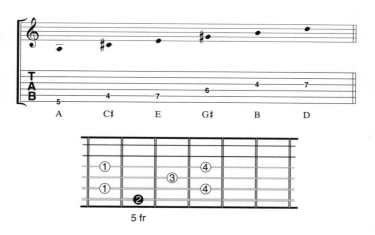

A major 11th arpeggio version 2   1 3 5 7 9 11

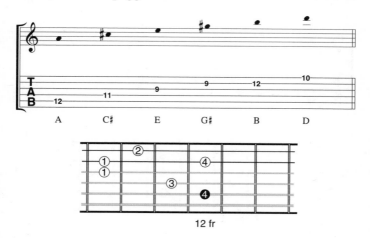

A minor 11th arpeggio version 1

1 ♭3 5 ♭7 9 11

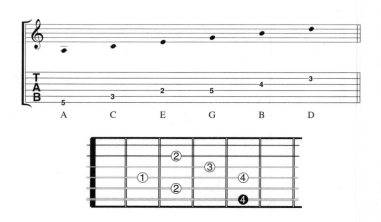

A minor 11th arpeggio version 2

1 ♭3 5 ♭7 9 11

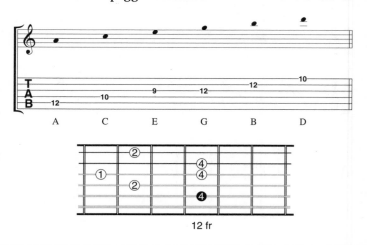

A dominant 13th arpeggio version 1   1 3 5 ♭7 9 11 13

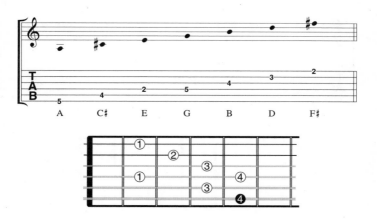

A dominant 13th arpeggio version 2   1 3 5 ♭7 9 11 13

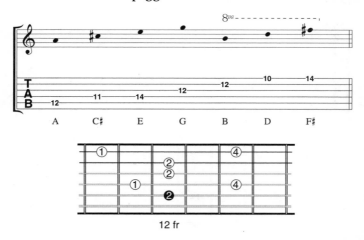

A major 13th arpeggio version 1

1 3 5 7 9 11 13

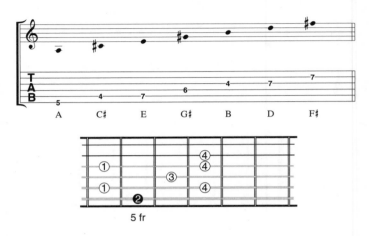

A major 13th arpeggio version 2

1 3 5 7 9 11 13

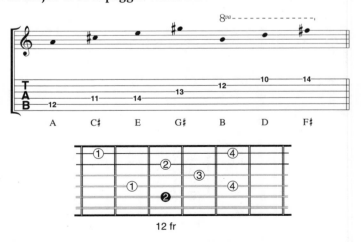

A minor 13th arpeggio version 1   1 ♭3 5 ♭7 9 11 13

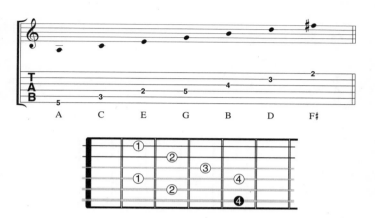

A minor 13th arpeggio version 2   1 ♭3 5 ♭7 9 11 13

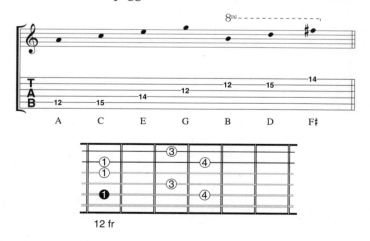

A dominant 7th ♯9 arpeggio

1 3 5 ♭7 ♯9

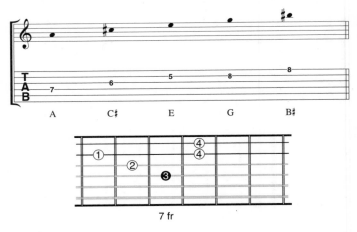

A dominant 7th ♭9 arpeggio

1 3 5 ♭7 ♭9

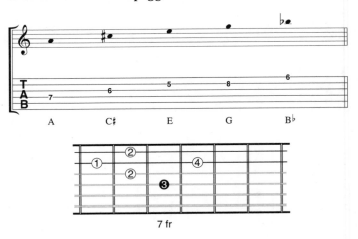

A dominant 7th ♯5 ♯9 arpeggio

1 3 ♯5 ♭7 ♯9

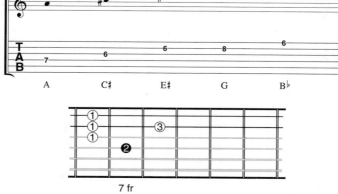

A   C♯   E♯   G   B♯

7 fr

A dominant 7th ♯5 ♭9 arpeggio

1 3 ♯5 ♭7 ♭9

A   C♯   E♯   G   B♭

7 fr

A dominant 7th ♭5 ♯9 arpeggio

1 3 ♭5 ♭7 ♯9

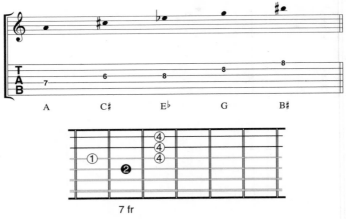

A dominant 7th ♭5 ♭9 arpeggio

1 3 ♭5 ♭7 ♭9

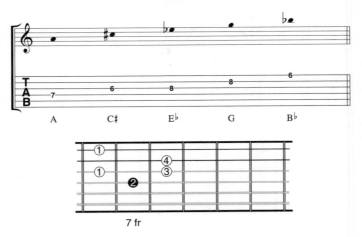

Exercises

When you can play a scale ascending and descending in its regular form, try it with these exercises. Each one breaks the notes up into different-sized fragments, helping you to think of each scale as a shape and a sound rather than a long string of notes. All, of course, can be played backwards when you get to the top of the scale. For simplicity, each exercise is shown using the notes of the easy major scale shape on page 9, but the idea can be applied to any scale.

Starting on page 60 there are seven musical examples, each featuring a chord sequence plus suggestions for which scale/arpeggio to use. For practice purposes, you could try recording the chord sequences as rhythm guitar parts, then try playing a solo over this backing track using the scale suggested.

Exercise 1: Up a 3rd - down a 2nd

Exercise 2: Up a 4th - down a 3rd

Exercise 3: Up a 4th - down a 2nd

Exercise 4: Up a 5th – down a 3rd

Exercise 5: Skipped 3rds

1. A major chord sequence (see pp. 9-11)

$\frac{4}{4}$ ‖: Amaj⁷ ╱ ╱ ╱ | F♯m ╱ ╱ ╱ | A ╱ Bm⁷ ╱ | Esus⁴ ╱ E ╱ |

| Dmaj⁷ ╱ ╱ ╱ | Amaj⁷ ╱ ╱ ╱ | Bm ╱ ╱ ╱ | Esus⁴ ╱ E ╱ :‖

A major scale shape

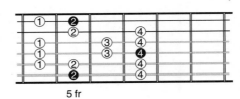

5 fr

2. A minor pentatonic chord sequence (see pp. 17-19)

$\frac{4}{4}$ ‖: Am ╱ ╱ ╱ | G ╱ ╱ ╱ | D ╱ ╱ ╱ | G ╱ ╱ ╱ |

| Am ╱ ╱ ╱ | Dm ╱ ╱ ╱ | F ╱ E⁷ ╱ | Am ╱ ╱ ╱ :‖

A minor pentatonic scale shape

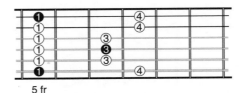

5 fr

3. A major pentatonic chord sequence (see pp. 20-22)

$\frac{4}{4}$ ‖: A / / / | / / / / | D / / / | / / / / |

| F#m / / / | D / / / | A / / / | E / / / :‖

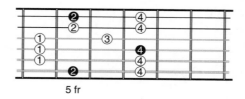

A major
pentatonic
scale shape

5 fr

4. A natural minor chord sequence (see pp. 13-16)

$\frac{4}{4}$ ‖: Am / / / | F / / / | Dm / / / | G / / / |

| Em / / / | G / / / | Am / / / | E / / / :‖

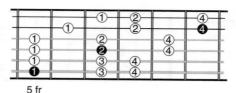

A natural
minor scale
shape

5 fr

Chord Sequences

Now try these sequences in keys other than A. Use the diagrams on page 4 to move the scale shapes you've learnt to the appropriate places on the fingerboard.

We've suggested a scale shape which would fit over each chord sequence, for soloing or playing melody lines. Why not try out some other chord sequence/scale combinations and see what you come up with!

5. E dorian mode chord sequence (see p. 24)

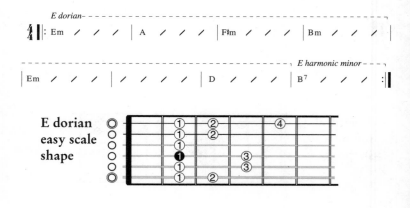

6. F♯ mixolydian mode chord sequence (see p. 24)

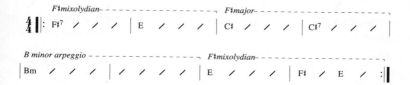

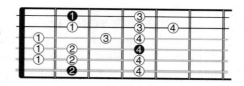

F♯
mixolydian
scale shape

7. 'Jazz' chord sequence (see p. 27)

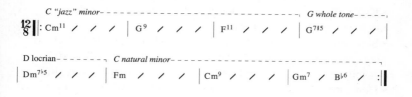

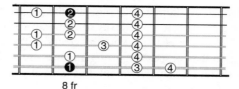

C 'jazz'
melodic
minor scale
shape

8 fr

Practice Tips

When you're learning guitar, you should aim to practise a little every day. Ideally, around a quarter of your practice time should be devoted to scales and arpeggios. The hints and tips on this page are designed to help you learn the scales with the minimum of effort, in the shortest time possible. They're not 'rules' (so feel free to ignore them!) but they should go a long way towards making your practice sessions more efficient.

BEFORE YOU START
• Ensure that your instrument – and your hands – are clean.
• Set up this book on a music stand, not the top of a chair. If your posture's wrong you won't be able to make any stretches in a scale.
• If you must stand up, don't have your guitar strap too long. A shortened strap may not look cool, but it sure makes the guitar easier to play.

WHEN YOU'RE PRACTISING
• Use a metronome if at all possible. It's a guaranteed way to improve evenness in your playing.
• Start slowly and build up to speed. You should aim to be able to play each scale at around 180 notes per minute (quavers at 90 beats per minute), but it's easier to start at half this speed or even slower.
• Don't just play a scale ascending and descending or you'll never be able to use it in a solo. Try the exercises on pages 57-59.
• If in doubt, use alternate picking with the plectrum (down-up-down-up etc) – this is a good way to maintain evenness.
• Don't feel you have to stick to one position. Try ascending using one position then descending using another, or shifting positions halfway through a scale. After all, this is what you'll be doing when you apply the scale to a piece of music.

7/05(55473)